Get the Hat
and
Dad Has a Nap

Written by
Robin Twiddy

Illustrated by
Alex Dingley &
Maia Batumashvili

Can you say this sound and draw it with your finger?

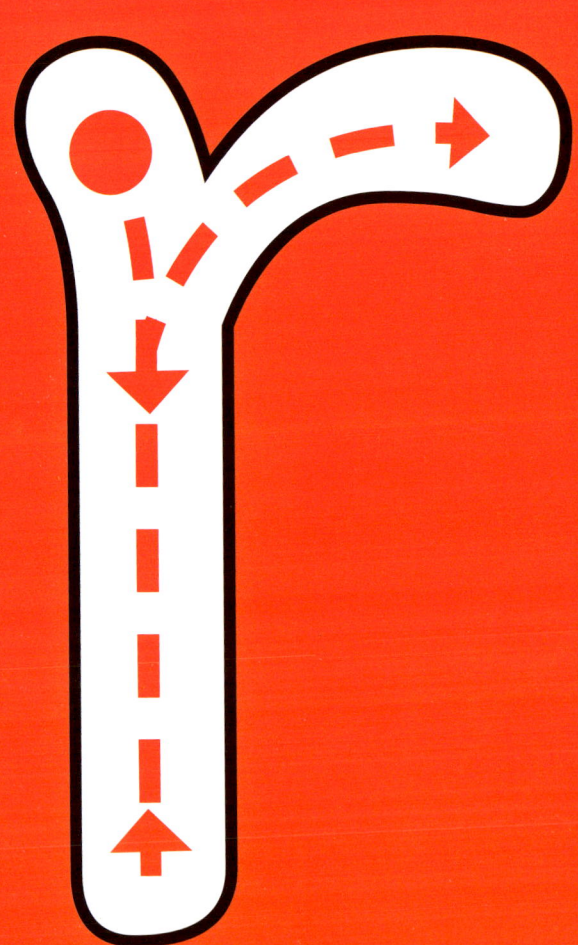

Get the Hat

Written by
Robin Twiddy

Illustrated by
Alex Dingley

It is Pat. Pat has a hat.

His hat is big and has bells.

A rat has got his hat!

The rat is in the hat.

Pat runs to get the hat. Puff, puff.

Get the hat, Pat! Duck.

Pat gets his cat, Tom.

Get the rat, Tom the cat!

The cat hit the hat.

The rat is on the mat!

Pat has got his hat back.

The cat has got the rat.

Can you say this sound and draw it with your finger?

Dad Has a Nap

Written by
Robin Twiddy

Illustrated by
Maia Batumashvili

Dad had a nap.

Tom had a fun plan.

Tom put a pen on Dad.

Tim put a man on Dad.

Tim put a bot on Dad.

Tom put a bug on Dad.

Tim put a hot pot on Dad.

It is fun!

Tom put the dog on Dad.

The pen, man and bot fell off.

The pot, bug and dog fell off.